Stars of American Ballet

A Photo Journal

All Rights Reserved

Copyright 2024 by Howard Dando

No part of this book may be reproduced or transmitted in any form or by any means, graphic, electronic, or mechanical, including photocopying, recording, taping, or by any information, storage, or retrieval systems, without the permission in writing from the author.

Information:
HowardDando7@gmail.com

Printed in the United States of America

Dedication

This photo journal serves as a tribute to the dancers featured within these pages, and all dancers who bring their beauty and joy to our world.

"To dance is to be out of yourself. Larger, more beautiful, more powerful. This is power, it is glory on earth and it is yours for the taking."

Agnes de Mille

"People have asked why I chose to be a dancer. I did not choose. I was chosen to be a dancer, and with that, you live all your life."

Martha Graham

Stars of American Ballet dancers on the front cover from top left and clockwise: Marianna Tcherkassky, Anna Maria D'Angelo, Patricia McBride, Fernando Bujones and Eleanor D'Antuono.

Dancer on the back cover: Phyllis Papa.

Stars of American Ballet created international headlines as the first Performing Arts Company to appear before multi-racial audiences during apartheid in South Africa.

Thereafter, Stars toured a record-breaking 66 American cities each year for the next three years.

The New York Times cited 'Stars' as "The resurgence of Balanchine's legendary 'Ballet Caravan."

Before you join us on the journey across the world, meet a few of the dancers on the tour.

From top and clockwise:
Hilda Morales,
Cynthia Harvey,
Linda Kuchera,
Marianna Tcherkassky.

Because of the major political event, newspapers in South Africa requested more photos.

We had only two hours for a shoot since the dancers were learning new ballets. None of the men were available, but a few ladies had a few minutes.

I had planned to shoot in color, but there was one black and white frame left in the camera.

Marianna Tcherkassky was the first out of the dressing room.

We made eye contact; but we did not say a word. I lifted my camera.

Marianna was 'on' in a second. It was the same with all the other dancers as when they left the wings to go on stage.

Marianna Tcherkassky was a principal dancer with the American Ballet Theatre, performing the lead in major classical and contemporary works.

The New York Times reviewed Marianna as "One of the greatest 'Giselle' that America has produced."

Marianna taught for the Bartholin Institute in Copenhagen, the University of Cincinnati.

She later became Ballet Mistress of Pittsburgh Ballet Theatre with her husband and Artistic Director, Terrence Orr.

We took three color shots with Marianna, and she rushed off to rehearsal.

Cynthia Harvey joined American Ballet Theatre and starred in almost every ballerina role.

Cynthia had the unique distinction of being the first and only American dancer invited by Sir Anthony Dowell to be a Principal Ballerina of The Royal Ballet.

Miss Harvey also performed as a guest artist with companies formed by Baryshnikov and Nureyev, as well as many other major ballet companies throughout the world.

Cynthia joined American Ballet in the corps at sixteen, but we recognized her talent and she became the youngest member of the Stars of American Ballet.

After Miss Harvey retired from American Ballet Theatre, she coached for the Australian Ballet, Royal Swedish Ballet, and La Scala Ballet.

Years later, Cynthia returned to ABT to become the Director of American Ballet Theatre's Jacqueline Kennedy Onassis School.

Since Cynthia was the youngest member of 'Stars', she had a shorter rehearsal schedule that allowed time for a few more photos.

She was also the only dancer who did not have her hair in a bun.

Memory does not recall whose idea it was to take a shot of Cynthia flinging her hair.

During this period, ballet programs were printed in black and white since color is expensive. But why not take the photographs in color, considering the souvenir program could convert to black and white?

Fortunately, and surprisingly, many of the newspapers printed the photos in color.

Most souvenir dance programs were quite formal, making it unusual to capture a photo of a dancer tossing her hair or tying toe shoes. However, why not experiment with a few unconventional poses?

Betty Chamberlain was a soloist with American Ballet Theatre.

Later, as a teacher, Betty trained students at NYU School of the Arts, Montclair State University, and Theatre Arts Dance America.

Betty retired because of dance-related injuries, but she later toured the country, winning many national awards in ballroom dancing.

Betty's rehearsals permitted just two poses.

Linda Kuchera was a soloist with American Ballet Theatre and Hamburg Ballet.

The process of shooting in film required several days for development, additional days for making prints, and even more time for shipping to South Africa.

Today a digital camera can take hundreds of shots in a few minutes, and sent around the world in a few seconds.

Despite the limitations, there is something personal and engaging in shooting in film.

The discovery of an old chair inspired a few Degas influenced poses.

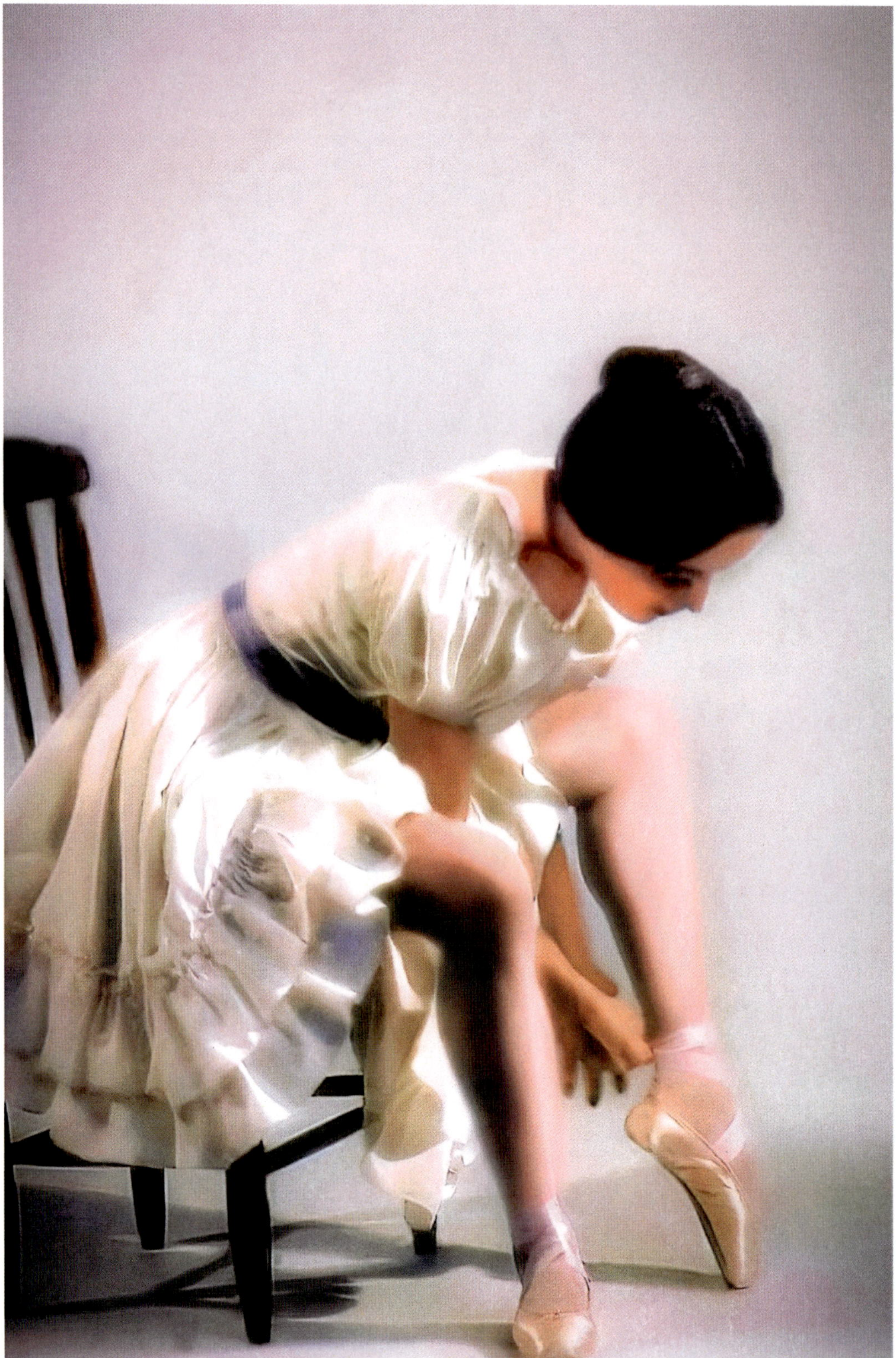

As Artistic Director, Hilda Morales was busy with rehearsals, and had only enough time for the group photo.

However, at a previous time, I suggested a Black Swan photo on a lake. It meant a long early morning drive to the Goldfarb farm, but Hilda agreed with the same spirit of adventure as with the journey to South Africa.

Miss Morales appeared in the film 'The Turning Point,' with Anne Bancroft and Shirley McLain, and on PBS in 'The Nutcracker.' She appeared as the 'Acid Queen in the original Broadway production at the New York City Center for the Who's rock opera 'Tommy' with Les Grands Ballets Canadians.

Hilda's relationship with Anthony Tudor was significant in presenting 'Stars' Professional World Premiere of 'Sunflowers.'

The ballet was later recognized as the basis for what would become Mr. Tudor's last ballet ('The Leaves are Fading.' Miss Morales recalled, "Mr. Tudor called me with a request to work with him...and it became the creation of his last ballet.

STARS TOUR SOUTH AFRICA ... *not without drama*.

The journey to South Africa involved a two-day, 20-hour flight with a layover in Paris. However, upon arrival in Paris, I received a telegram informing me that our visas had been revoked.

The night in Paris was frantic with calls and telegrams. It was not until the next morning, less than two hours before our scheduled flight, that our visas had been restored. The company quickly gathered in the lobby and then dashed to the airport in just minutes to board our scheduled flight.

Most of the South African government eagerly supported Stars performing before their first multi-racial audience - but regrettably, not everyone was on board.

We landed on September 1, 1975; the newspaper photo expressed our joy to land on the African tarmac; although we did not expect to be met by the press at the airport or later at our hotel. After all, we were not the Beatles but had not yet realized that Stars was to be international front-page news for breaking the country's racial barriers.

DIE BURGER, MAANDAG, 1 SEPTEMBER 1975

STARS OF THE AMERICAN BALLET, 'n geselskap van dansers van 'n paar Amerikaanse balletgeselskappe, het gistermiddag op die lughawe D. F. Malan aangekom. Hulle sal twee verskillende programme in Kaapstad aanbied: die eerste van 1 tot 3 September en die tweede van 4 tot 6 September. Heel links op die foto staan mnr. David Poole, balletmeester van KRUIK, en langs hom is die twee hoofdansers, Violette Verdi en Helgi Tomasson.

Newspaper photo

During our month of performances, both English and African language newspapers printed 'double-truck' (two full-facing pages) in full color.

Ballet photos in color are a rarity in American newspapers, and it is even more extraordinary for major American newspaper to dedicate two full-color pages to ballet. But South African newspapers ran daily reviews with color photos that even appeared on the front pages.

International coverage, especially European newspapers, was also extensive, but ironically, hardly covered by the American press.

We were aware of a previous three-month tour in South Africa with the Royal Ballet. The Royal Ballet did one performance for an exclusive all-black audience that was reviewed in the press as an "insult' and "shabby." That one performance featured only excerpts of ballets, provided no sets, and "took place in a drab city municipal hall rather than a proper theatre." The Royal Ballet also excluded its only dancer of color from the tour. The Royal Ballet's engagement took place during the Sharpeville massacre on March 21, 1960. From a peaceful protest, the event erupted as the police fired bullets into the crowd, wounding 180 people and killing 69.

We were aware of the history, but for the Stars tour, there were no riots, protests, or pickets. In contrast, every show was completely sold out and received standing ovations, along with rave reviews from the press, radio, and television.

Immediately after the 'Stars' tour, the government passed legislation that "All forthcoming theatre events would be performed in front of all races." Stars felt honored to contribute to a significant milestone in the progression of international civil rights.

'SUNFLOWERS,' A WORLD PREMIER

Most dance critics would agree the three most important ballet chorographers of the twentieth century were Balanchine, Frederick Ashton and Antony Tudor.

It was a great honor to perform the world premiere of a Tudor work.

'Sunflowers' began with two young girls joyfully playing in a field on a summer's day.

The two girls are joined by a friend.

They meet with another friend on what promises to be a perfect day.

Two young men enter the field to flirt with the girls.

One girl is enchanted by the young man's attention, but her girlfriend is jealous and turns away.

After flirting, the boy tries to leave, but the girl tries to stop him.

Rejected, the girl leaves in tears.

Another girl competes for the attention of the other boy.

The boy flirts, but then tosses her aside.

Eventually, both boys lose interest and walk away. The earlier gentle melodies are transformed into strident music; and the once soft lighting turns harsh.

The girls are left with a new understanding of their competition and the drastic change in their relationships.

Alan Peterson of Dance Magazine described 'Sunflowers' as "A piece that must be savored a few times to appreciate its subtlety and delicate beauty."

South African critics praised the work, but some audience members expressed difficulty with the stringent contemporary music of Janacek's 'String Quartet.

The 'Kreutzer Sonata' was inspired by a Tolstoy novella protesting maltreatment toward women, and the Tolstoy's novella was inspired by Beethoven's Violin Sonata No.9, 'The Kreutzer.'

'Sunflowers' is considered the inspiration for Anthony Tudor's final work 'Leaves are Fading,' which premiered years later by American Ballet Theatre (with Baryshnikov).

Ironically, the original ABT cast of 'Leaves are Fading' included members of 'Stars of American Ballet' who had appeared in 'Sunflowers' in South Africa."

Anna Kisselgoff in the New York Times reviewed Stars' American premiere of 'Sunflowers' as "A marvelous idea for presenting the complex and challenging work."

FREE DAYS

On one of the non-matinee days, we took advantage of a sightseeing trip to the southern tip of South Africa.

Marianna was smiling, but near tears as she viewed the primordial scenery.

The absence of civilization was striking; there were no familiar landmarks, not a fast-food chain for miles, no housing or commercial establishments in sight, only a narrow dirt road that meandered towards the ocean.

It was an opportunity to witness the Earth as it existed millions of years ago.

Our travel guide related Cape Point was the meeting point of two oceans, the Atlantic and Indian; but that was not accurate. The actual area where the two oceans meet was nearby at Cape Agulhas.

Our guide also mentioned that the icy waters were almost as cold as the Antarctic, and the fish included great white sharks.

Many consider dancers to be among the greatest athletes on the planet, but none of our dancers volunteered to climb down the steep rugged mountain for a dip in the icy, shark-infested waters.

In this primeval beauty, a horde of unfriendly indigenous inhabitants arrived.

Our guide warned us, but out of nowhere, a dozen baboons charged down from the mountain to try and snatch handbags, jewelry, and food.

Our guide hurriedly opened the center panels of our Kombi (a van) for the dancers. They screamed and jumped in the van, piling on top of each other as if performing amazing ballet 'fish dives.' (It still brings a smile to memory.)

On the way back to Cape Town, we were struck by the juxtaposition of the breathtaking view of Table Top Mountain and a disturbing sign, a reminder of a purpose of the tour.

Helgi Tomasson feeds a couple of baby elephants before we set off on our safari

During our safari, we saw animals in the 'wild,' although the giraffes were so used to tourists that I fed cookies to a giraffe through the window of our jeep. We tried to come close to camels and ostriches, but they dashed away. However, we stayed in our jeep, far away from the lions.

On another non-matinee day, Betty Chamberlain had fun with a statue at Zoo Park, on the outskirts of Johannesburg. Some dancers visited Soweto to see the sad effects of apartheid.

During other free afternoons, the company went souvenir shopping. While South Africa is famous for diamonds, we chose not to purchase 'The Star of Africa' but bought less expensive gems and jewelry, including crystal geodes, aquamarine, amethyst, turquoise, and native African woodwork.

South African restrictions forbid taking Krugerrands back to the United States. During that time, the price of one gold Krugerrand was $35 dollars. If we could have kept just one Krugerrand coin, it would now be worth $1,990.

The Johannesburg marque seemed half of a city block, and at night could be seen a half mile away. Years after our tour, the elegant Her Majesty's theatre, an example of turn-of-the-century architecture, was demolished for a shopping center.

Before our departure for the South African tour, some people expressed concern about the challenges of navigating through the deep, dark jungles of Africa.

Quite the opposite, Johannesburg is a major global business hub, surpassing New York and London in size.

Hotel accommodations were excellent; food was beyond expectations; and South African wines competed with the vineyards of France and California.

However, there was one incident where we were invited to a typical South African lunch. The host insisted I try a seasoning on one dish. It was hotter than hell. He then handed me a glass or water. That made it even hotter. It was noted later that it was the hottest pepper on the planet.

We left the high altitude and thin air of Johannesburg for Cape Town. Our hotel was unique in that it was built into ocean rocks. At night, the surf splashed against our windows, but the undulating sound made it easy to fall asleep.

All the dancers struggled for weeks with the thin air of Johannesburg with an elevation of 5,751 feet, but once arriving in Cape Town, the dancers were jumping to the ceiling.

In the above photo, Cynthia Harvey's trailing leg was almost equal to Linda Kuchera's shoulders.

I knew Cynthia's 'jete' was coming in 'Laurencia Pas de Six' and fortunately had my camera. But I had to take the shot from the back of the theatre that was very far from the stage, and no telephoto lens, so later I had to severely crop the photo, but just enough to catch Cynthia's jump.

With all the shows completely sold out, there was no chance to record from the audience, but only to take photos from the wings.

Our South Africa repertoire was mostly classical, but it was important to introduce contemporary American modern works such as, 'After Eden.'

The ballet told the story of Adam and Eve. Dancers, Keith Martin and Hilda Morales intertwining their bodies around each other in what seemed impossible contortions, and was startling erotic.

Critics were captivated by the modern work: "It was a risk to place classical and modern pieces on the same program, but it paid handsome dividends resulting in spectacular ballet South African balletomanes will remember for a long time."

Marika Bender, The Cape Times

Keith Martin was principal dancer with the Royal Ballet, Pennsylvania Ballet, Pittsburgh Ballet Theatre, San Francisco Ballet, and Maryland Ballet. He was the director of San Diego Ballet, and Director of the Phoenix Ballet Company, Ballet California, and Ballet Indiana. In film and television, Mr. Martin is known for 'The Tales of Beatrix Potter,' 'The Dream,' and 'The Nutcracker.'

John Butler, the choreographer of 'After Eden', was a former member of the Martha Graham Company and appeared on Broadway as Dream Curly in the original Broadway production of Oklahoma! He created works for Broadway, New York City Opera, Alvin Ailey American Dance Theater, American Ballet Theatre, Harkness, Metropolitan Opera, New York City Ballet, Paris Opera Ballet, Pennsylvania Ballet, and the Royal Winnipeg Ballet. His 'Carmina Burana' was performed by over 30 other companies.

I asked Mr. Butler how he could connect with family and friends as he choreographed across the world for 50 weeks a year; he responded that he always placed photos of family and friends in every hotel room to keep them in his heart.

SHOW MAIL

Rock man of Ballet

DORA SOWDEN

NEW YORK is now ballet-mad. Going to the ballet has become "utterly fashionable" — so much so that not going is a form of becoming "declassé". So says Howard Dando, producer of "Stars of the American Ballet", now appearing in Johannesburg and soon going to Cape Town.

"The seasons of the American Ballet Theatre and the New York City Ballet are sold out long before they start," he told me, "and it's no longer only the women who go, as it used to be seven or eight years ago. Men bring their dates."

He attributes this change to the effect of visits of Russian ballet companies.

"Until a decade ago, Americans considered ballet sissified. Then they began to see what athletes the men were. This produced a drastic change not only in dancers, but in audiences."

Overloaded

Today, the American companies — and not only the New York City Ballet and American Ballet Theatre — are "overloaded with talent". That is why some of the dancers join other companies during vacation time and go on summer tours in the States and abroad.

That is how the "Stars" company is able to travel and was able to come here.

One of the pleasures of travel was making acquaintance with audience reaction of various kinds, said Mr Dando.

"We're used to curtain calls that make curtain-raising necessary again and again. 'Don Quixote' usually gets 25 minutes of ovation. Then we realised that South African audiences were different.

"Also in New York, we have half-hour intermissions because the audiences like to be social and gossip about the dancers. Here we found that the audiences got nervous if the intervals are too long."

Yet he and the dancers have found the audiences here "rather refreshing". They want to come again. "Next time we'll be a bigger company," he said.

Though he looks like a teenager, Howard Dando is 31, and already has 10 years of theatre experience behind him. He took his master's degree in drama — and his "first love" is still "legitimate theatre".

He was the director on Broadway of "Tommy" (now filmed) and of "Sgt. Pepper's Lonely Hearts Club Band" (with Beatles music). He has an interest in a "Rock" magazine. He is also co-owner of a theatre "entirely devoted to Rock music", which, he says has undergone great transformation and is now more sophisticated and more melodic too.

Mr Dando was co-founder of the American Dance Festival in Philadelphia.

"We now bring six different companies for one week's residence each season", he said. "During that time they perform also in schools".

The festival gets support from the state, the city and the schools.

The "Stars" company that Howard Dando has brought here was carefully selected. Size had something to do with the choice of dancers because he wanted them to match well.

HOWARD DANDO . . . a drastic change in attitudes.

"They also had to be versatile and to have good personality".

South Africans, said Mr Dando, seem to be unfamiliar with modern ballet. When he was sitting in the audience during the performance of John Butler's "After Eden", he heard a woman behind him say, after three minutes: "Harry, what's going on here".

Yet this showed him the field could be developed and that South African audiences were ready for this kind of ballet "education"

John Lennon, rehearsal 'Sgt. Pepper's.'

We assumed requests for interviews from the press and radio would fade after the first week in Johannesburg, but the press continued until the last performance.

Media was also interested in the contrast of my background in rock concerts and Producer of the original Broadway production of the Who's rock opera 'Tommy' with Les Grands Ballet Canadiens.

'Tommy' toured for two years with three return engagements in New York. When I first negotiated the rights, the attorney was surprised how I could make a rock album into a musical. I explained 'Tommy' was a narrative. Although the merger seemed improbable at first, but ballet and rock music can tell a story.

Years later, I became a producer of the Broadway production of the Beatles 'Sgt. Pepper's Lonely Hearts Club Band.' It did not have a strong narrative, but it was great fun. Unfortunately, the same cannot be said for the film adaptation.

Unfortunately, my once unique idea of turning the rock album 'Tommy' into a theatre work may have inspired an overabundance of Broadway shows based on pop albums, and lessened the number of 'original' musicals composed for the theatre, and comedies and dramas now playing on Broadway. Sorry!

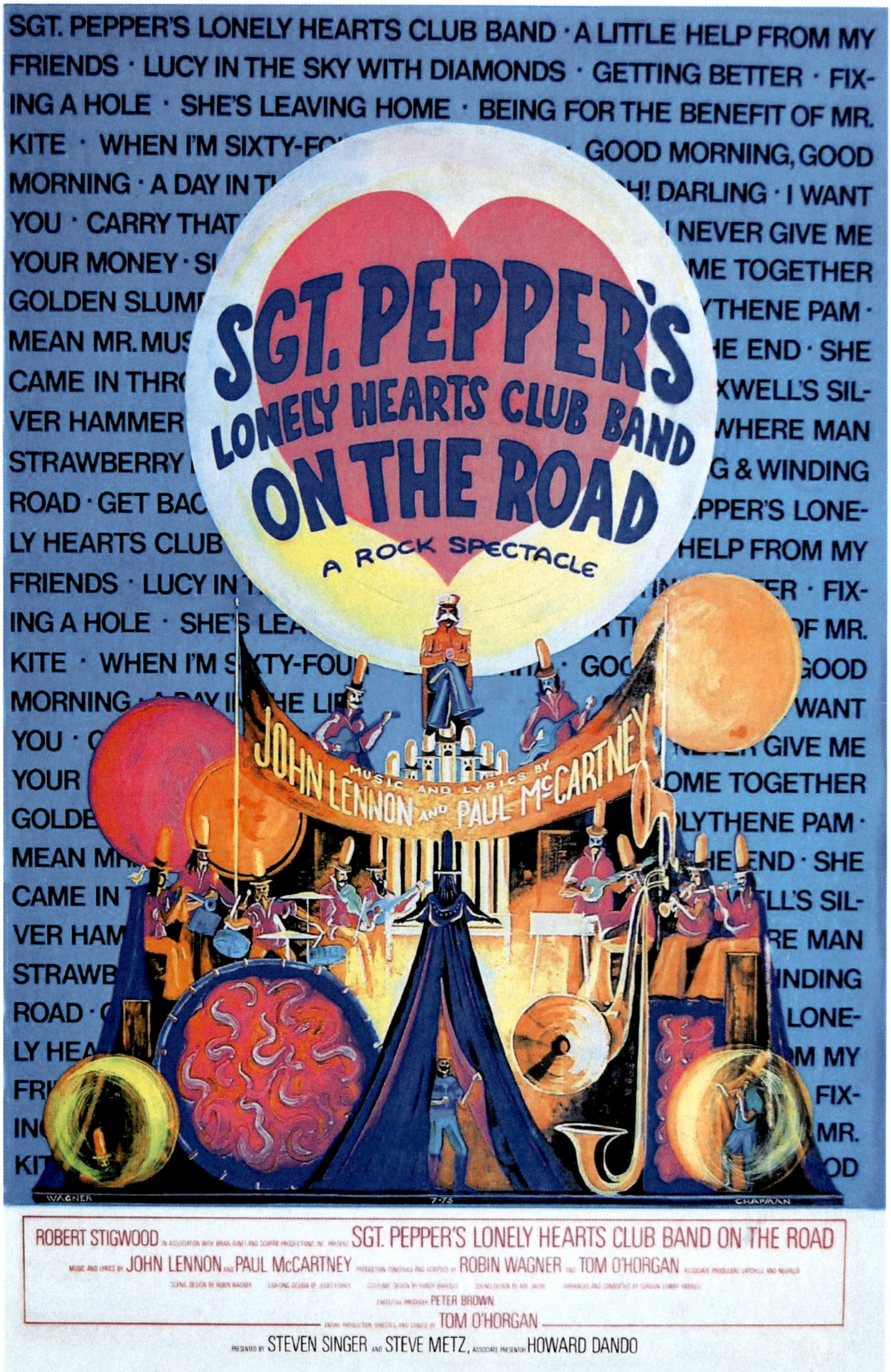
SGT. PEPPER'S LONELY HEARTS CLUB BAND · A LITTLE HELP FROM MY FRIENDS · LUCY IN THE SKY WITH DIAMONDS · GETTING BETTER · FIXING A HOLE · SHE'S LEAVING HOME · BEING FOR THE BENEFIT OF MR. KITE
SGT. PEPPER'S
LONELY HEARTS CLUB BAND
ON THE ROAD
A ROCK SPECTACLE
MUSIC AND LYRICS BY
JOHN LENNON AND PAUL McCARTNEY
WAGNER
7-75
CHAPMAN
ROBERT STIGWOOD SGT. PEPPER'S LONELY HEARTS CLUB BAND ON THE ROAD
JOHN LENNON PAUL McCARTNEY ROBIN WAGNER TOM O'HORGAN
PETER BROWN
TOM O'HORGAN
PRESENTED BY STEVEN SINGER AND STEVE METZ, ASSOCIATE PRESENTOR HOWARD DANDO

Marianna Tcherkassky and Kirk Peterson in Swan Lake

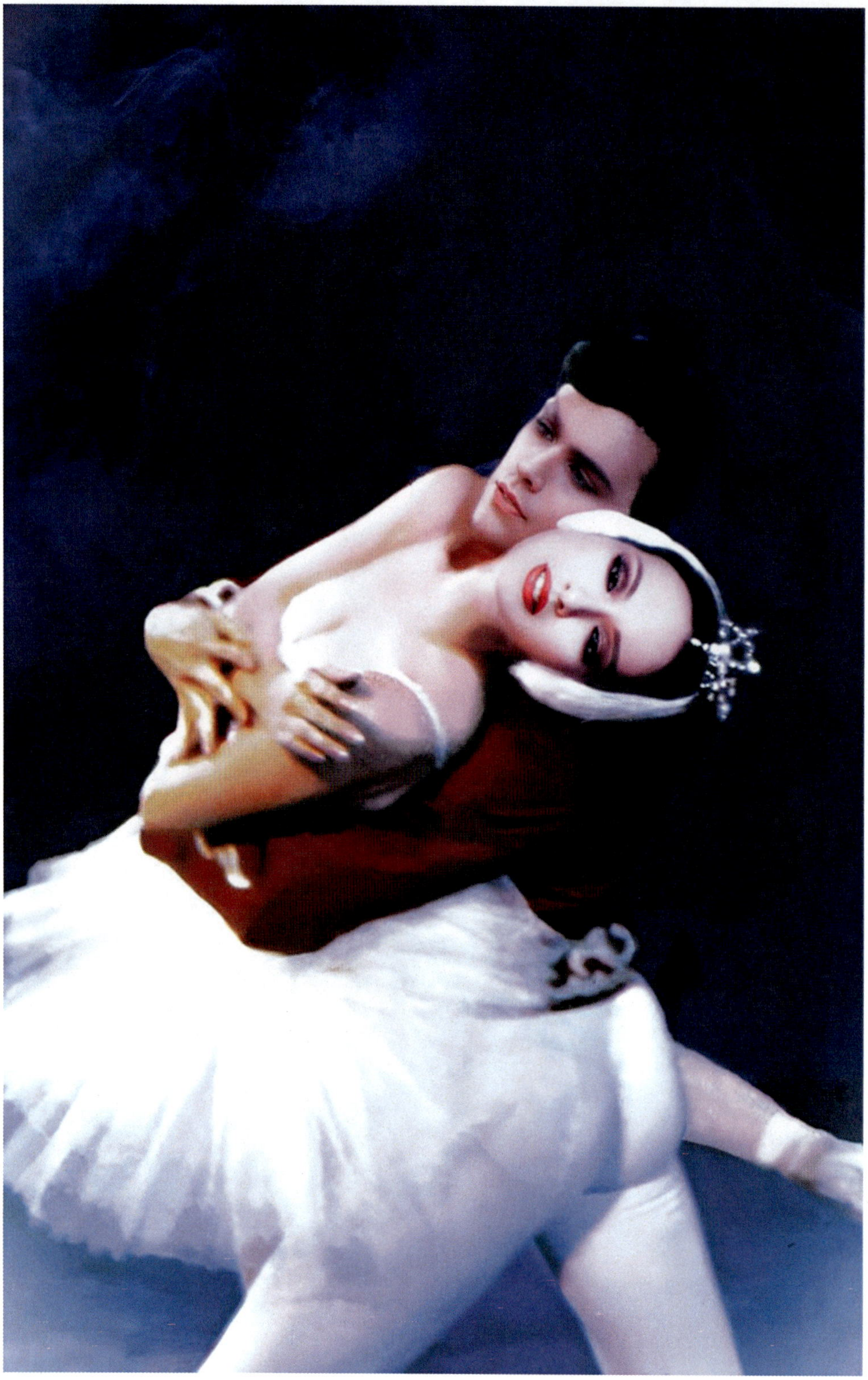

Despite official government policy, most people in South Africa were not as radical as some had assumed.

Despite initial worries about safety, our efforts to challenge racial discrimination were met with overwhelming support from audiences, the public, and the media. It was inspiring to see people unite behind our performing for multi-racial audiences.

Prior to the last performance in South Africa, Cynthia Harvey was deep in thought while stretching on the barre.

I later caught Cynthia and Linda having a 'toe talk.'

Both dancers were oblivious as I snapped the photo while walking out of the studio.

Most of our dancers have never seen their pictures in this journal until this publication. In the past, it was much more difficult to send and distribute photos.

(Some photos in this journal are on the Fine Arts América website.)

THE FINAL CURTAIN IN SOUTH AFRICA

After our final curtain, Helgi Tomasson took a moment to stretch out on the stage floor.

The ladies of the company had the inspiration to pile their curtain call flowers on top of Helgi; one dancer even contributed a leg warmer.

Helgi's talent was highly respected by everyone on the tour. Not only was he a remarkable dancer with impeccable technique, but he also embodied elegance and was always supportive and cooperative, regardless of the tour's difficulties. It was an honor and a pleasure to have Helgi on Stars tours for the next several years.

At 17 Helgi was discovered by Jerome Robbins, who arranged a scholarship at the School of American Ballet. Helgi also danced with Joffrey Ballet and Harkness Ballet, and 15 years as a Principal with New York City Ballet. Helgi is currently the Artistic Director of the San Francisco Ballet.

NEXT STOP OVER: CANNES

After the flight from South Africa, our stop-over landed us in the land of the rich and famous. We headed straight to the beach. It was early September but so cool and windy that Marianna, Cynthia, and Betty had to wrap themselves in their Air France blankets.

The following day was warmer, so Marianna could soak up some rays, but kept her blanket nearby, just in case.

Somehow Marianna found a dress that matched the beach umbrellas!

Marianna caught me checking out a Rolls Royce outside our hotel.

Later that night, we went for dinner at the Hotel de Paris. I escorted four beautiful and elegantly dressed ladies that drew stares from other diners who may have wondered who was this guy surrounded by so many dazzling beautiful ladies.

After dinner, our server related that a special dessert had been prepared for us. We graciously declined. But our server responded the chef was a ballet fan and recognized our ballerinas; and that his signature dessert was usually only made for presidents and royalty.

We appreciated the honor and the kindness and agreed; and assumed the portions would be small, but the server brought two huge raspberry souffles. We agreed among ourselves to be polite and take small bites, but the dessert was so delicious that we finished both souffles.

We asked the server if we could thank the chef, but the server returned with the message from the chef that it was enough of a pleasure and honor to have such artists at his restaurant. After dinner, we took a short walk to the Casino de Monte Carlo.

Some gentlemen wore tuxedos, and most of the ladies were attired in the latest Parisian couture. There was polite applause if someone won a big bet, unlike the whoops and hollers at the Vegas casinos. I watched one gentleman lose ten thousand dollars, but his reaction was only to adjust his bow tie and most likely returned to his yacht in the harbor. The experience had the unreal feeling of being in a James Bond movie.

STARS, THE USA PREMIERE

A few months after the South African tour, Stars premiered in the United States with our South African company, but adding Patricia McBride, who danced with Helgi Tomasson.

Patricia McBride joined the New York City Ballet in 1959, where she spent nearly 30 years.

Miss McBride was awarded the prestigious Kennedy Center Honors, an honor given for lifetime contributions to American culture.

It was an honor to have Miss McBride on many of our national tours.

Westchester Weekend

FRIDAY DECEMBER 5, 1975 Volume 2, Number 35

Stars of American Ballet... See Page 3

The premiere performance in America quickly sold out at a large theater, a glowing review from The New York Times; and sponsorship by the National Endowment for the Arts provided the impetus to establish the company for national tours.

But we never expected the staggering schedule of performing in 66 cities each year in the only the fall and spring seasons.

We immediately began casting for new company dancers for our first American tour.

Phyllis was quickly selected as the new Artistic Director.

Miss Papa was formerly with American Ballet Theatre, Harkness Ballet, and with the Royal Danish Ballet to become the first American to be accepted into the company.

We needed black and white headshots for programs and press for the first American tour.

But a soft autumn light streamed into the beautiful Harkness studios that inspired more artistic shots. I switched to color.

Phyllis Papa, Harkness Studios, New York City.

By late afternoon, the light in the studio gradually dimmed, casting a soft fading glow.

After the natural light faded, we took a few black-and-white photographs before ending the shoot.

The American Tours

Most major American cities had tourist magazines in hotel rooms with covers of our upcoming performances.

However, we hardly had time to read the magazine articles since we went directly from the airports, dropped our luggage at the hotels, and headed for the theatres.

When we played 'one-nighters', we did not have enough time to fully unpack and lived out of our suitcases.

Traveling the country to play 66 cities a year did not allow a luxury of time with the logistics of moving between airplanes, taxis, buses, hotels, and theatres. There was hardly room in the luggage for camera equipment, or the luxury of time to take photos on tours. Unfortunately, I did not take a photo for the next three years of the tour.

Most of our downtime was on airplanes where Suzanne Farrell and I would do the New York Times crossword puzzles. A competition was proposed. Fortunately, I heard Suzanne could finish a puzzle in five minutes. I graciously declined the challenge.

Instead, during our flights, I began writing a novel on many yellow legal pads. Years later, my fiction novel of the fierce competition of dancers was published.

Most program covers featured our marquee names; however, occasionally local artists designed covers, such as this beautiful program by Houston artist D. Lavenner.

Children Matinees

Stars performed 'Peter and the Wolf' for Children's Matinees; together with a lecture demonstration that brought children on stage with our dancers.

Stars also provided Master Classes with our Stars for high school and college dance students.

The article mentions a traffic jam caused by our Children's Matinee and a teacher's 50-mile journey with a bus full of kids.

God bless that teacher!

Our shows often made front-page news; however, it was surprising for children's matinees and especially printed in color.

Free Press Photo by ELAINE ISAACSON

PETER, RIGHT, DANCES WITH THE BIRD IN 'PETER AND THE WOLF' BALLET MATINEE
... the excellent 20-minute performance

By MAGGIE MAURICE
Free Press Lifestyles Editor

There was a traffic jam on Main Street Thursday afternoon. Kids everywhere. Cops directing traffic. "What on earth is going on here?" a man asked.

The Stars of the American Ballet were doing Prokofiev's children's classic "Peter and the Wolf" in Memorial Auditorium.

Every seat was taken. Teachers and parents and children — some

A Review

Professional is as professional does, especially star 'stars' McBride and Tomasson..................**Page 16C**

from 50 miles away — were there to see it.

Outside there were buses from Harwood Union, Vergennes Elementary School. Mothers with cars full of children were driving around the block looking for a place to park.

Inside, there was no chaos. The teachers had prepared the children for what they were about to see. An air of controlled excitement went through the auditorium.

The Burlington Free Press
A GANNETT NEWSPAPER
Vermont's Largest... Most Quoted!

151st Year Serving Vermont • Four Sections, 20¢ — No. 308 • Friday, November 4, 1977

Good Morning, Vermont

70-Degree Day Sets a Record

Jackets slung over shoulders and rolled-up shirtsleeves were the order of the day Thursday when the mercury climbed to a record-breaking 70 degrees at 3 p.m. The previous high on Nov. 3 had been 68 degrees in 1936. Today's forecast calls for a chance of showers......**Page 2A**

Soccer Game Goes Into 25 Overtimes

CENTERVILLE, Ohio (AP) — The longest high school soccer match in national history ended Thursday night when Centerville defeated Dayton Carroll 2-1 in the 25th overtime on a shot with seven seconds left in the period.

The marathon game, extending over two nights, topped the previous national record of 21 overtime soccer periods set in 1974 by California teams

Wolf on the Prowl

The fearful beast in 'Peter and the Wolf,' portrayed by Sergio Cal of The Stars of the American Ballet, stalks across Memorial Auditorium in Burlington before a capacity crowd of youngsters at a special matinee Thursday. Columnist Maggie Maurice reports **Page 1C**.

Free Press Photo by ELAINE ISAACSON

As I stood on the stage, narrating 'Peter and the Wolf', it was a joy to watch the young audience's faces light up with delight and amazement.

In addition, we provided Master Classes, Lecture Demonstrations, and radio and television interviews when we played a city for several days.

One of the 'one-nighters' was in Grinnell, Iowa, with a population of only 9,500 residents.
As I recall, there were only three hotels, and ours was in the middle of a cow field. I would guess there were more cows than people. Nevertheless, the performance was completely sold out at the high school auditorium.

If there was a purpose for the US Dance Touring Program to bring the arts to the people of America beyond the big cities. This was it! I do not know how Grinnell did it. Bravo!

Our one-night stops did not allow time for children's matinees. That inspired an idea to create a TV pilot to provide instructions to young dancers across the country. A second part of the program of interviews with professional dancers. After we shot the pilot, we realized the program was better with only the interviews, but we also realized that time was consumed by our touring schedule.

For a TV pilot, I interviewed Violette Verdy. Her charm is available on YouTube:

https://www.youtube.com/watch? v=x1r040Cbmto&t=13s

The world loved Violette; but on the African tour, I couldn't resist pulling a practical joke: Violette was on stage for rehearsal; and I was in the sound booth and explained that we had a problem that required changing a tempo.

Violette, always cooperative, replied, "No problem." Violette began dancing to the accompaniment of an amateur orchestra, characterized by screechy violins and a funereal tempo.

After a few seconds, she stopped and shouted, "Howard, what the hell?" She was surrounded by laughter from the dancers who were all in on the joke. Violette appreciated the fun, and it unified the company in that we were all in this together.

As a tribute to Violette, we included a Special Note in every program during our last tour.

"The tour is dedicated to Violette Verdy, the ballerina who premiered at Stars of American Ballet's first performance and who appeared with Stars for the last performance of her career."

STARS OF AMERICAN BALLET PRODUCTION STAFF

Director and Founder .... Howard Dando
Artistic Director .... Paul Mejia
Lighting Designer/Stage Manager .... Paul Lindsay Butler
Administrative Manager .... Cameron Harper
Resident Set and Costume Designer .... Rick Paul
Costume and Headpiece Construction .... George Potts
Legal .... Robert Kline, Esq.
Special Counsel .... Warner and Gilles
Accounting .... Michael Pagano and Co.
Costumes .... Grace Costumes;
Orfe Costumes
Sound .... Hagen's Sound, Inc.
Rehearsal Pianist .... Linda Pelrine
Teachers .... Vicky Simon, Sara Leland,
Airie Henninger, Paul Russell
Transportation .... Troubador Travel, Inc.
Tour Direction .... Barry Weissler,
National Artists Management Co.,
165 W. 46th St., N.Y.C., N.Y.
212 - 575-1044

SPECIAL NOTE: The 1977-1978 tour is dedicated to Violette Verdy, the ballerina who premiered at Stars of American Ballet's first performance and who appeared with Stars of American Ballet for the last performance of her career.

Photo: Suzanne Farrell

Ballet with the Buffalo Philharmonic

Colleges and Universities

Many performances took place at colleges and universities, particularly those renowned for robust arts programs like the North Carolina School of the Arts.

But we were often pleasantly surprised by the number of bookings from schools that were not typically associated with the arts, or more famous for its football or basketball programs.

The heartland of the mid-west had many outstanding theaters with enthusiastic ballet fans who welcomed us with open arms, impressing us with their ballet knowledge.

College student bodies were most enthusiastic and commented on how they were astonished and excited to see ballet live and not have to watch on a small television screen.

It was also most common for student news staff to request permission to photograph our dancers.

Shall we dance?   O'Collegian staff photo by Steve Castleberry

Stars of the American Ballet, Kay Mazzo and Helgi Thomasson, entertain with a "pas de deux" in a private rehearsal before the company's opening Tuesday night. The final performance of the touring ballet will be Wednesday at 8 p.m.

Critics

A ballet experience would not be complete without reading newspaper reviews the next morning. Oscar Wilde is famously quoted, "The critic is one who knows the price of everything and the value of nothing." But in years of touring, it was the opposite.

Our experience revealed that critics were not only appreciative - but also supportive. The review below is an example.

Kent, McBride Shine Bright In Stars Ballet

By Helen C. Smith
Constitution Staff Writer

If only dance were not so ephemeral. There are some moments that are so exquisite that you wish you could hang onto them for ever.

Such was the will-o'-the wisp delight of Allegra Kent's performance Sunday during the Stars of the American Ballet's second concert at the Fox Theatre this weekend presented by the Atlanta Ballet.

Partnered by the handsome and ever empathetic Jacques D'Amboise, Miss Kent enraptured the audience with her weightless, delicate interpretation in the "Meditation" pas de deux, a work choreographed by D'Amboise. It is a lovely piece, a nice blending of the disembodied classical expressions for passion with more sensual ones known on earth.

The pair also danced the "Scotch Symphony" pas de deux with that same flow between them they exhibited in "Meditation" that creates those special moments of wonderment on stage. In some of the lifts, Miss Kent looked as if she were floating, without support, through the air, so effortless did it seem for both her and D'Amboise. They flirted with their fingertips, their hands, their arms, sometimes touching, sometimes just missing. They melted into each other's arms with their eyes, even when they were a stage width apart.

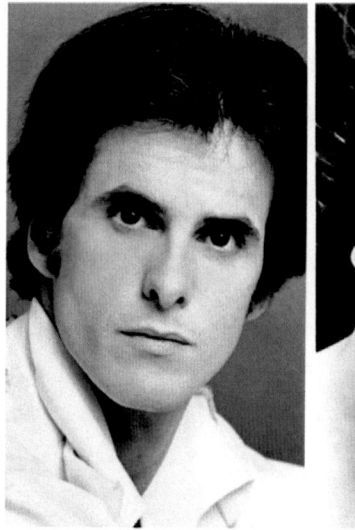

The night before Patricia McBride was the charmer. Each ballerina creates her own special magic. Miss McBride punctuates her own style of lyricism with sudden little snaps of fire.

Miss McBride and Helgi Tomasson danced the "Who Cares" pas de deux, music by Gershwin, choreography by Balanchine; and the Tchaikovsky pas de deux, with choreography again by Balanchine. Tomasson was best in the first number. He was all macho to her softness,

Helgi Tomasson   **Patricia McBride**

(The following section of this review is enlarged on the next page to be easier to read.)

Dance

On Saturday, the most intriguing piece was "7 & 7," to the music of Stravinsky with choreography by Paul Mejia, the artistic director of the company.

The music is discordant, full of tricky rhythms, sometimes trying, yet the choreography fits it very well. The title means that seven dancers perform to seven pieces of music. Two men (Thomas Banasiak and Richard Lee) seem to be trying to get a manequin (Lisa Moon) to do their bidding. On the other hand, sometimes it looks as if she is manipulating them. They arrange her legs and arms as if she were a doll, and then those same legs and arms lift and kick and arabesque on their own. The piece is characterized by some bizarre lifts and stretches, the point of which seems to be to achieve the longest possible limb extension of the manequin until she looks spread on a rack. For all that, it has wit in it, more so than any other work performed.

Too often, it seems, we forget our own and turn out in droves (over 5,000 saw the two performances of the Stars of the American Ballet this weekend) for the New York import.

Miss Smith's opening line of the review is superb, "If only dance were not so ephemeral. There are some moments that you wish you could hang onto forever."

Miss Smith's acknowledgement of choreographer Paul Mejia's recent ballet as the "most intriguing performance" was remarkable, since she showed courage by praising Mr. Mejica's work compared to the level of Balanchine's works. Bravo!

Miss Smith also observed Stars had full houses for two performances, attracting an audience of over 5,000. However, she also urges her community to show their support for the local Atlanta Ballet. Ironically, the sponsor of the Stars event was Atlanta Ballet that was to help raise money for Atlanta Ballet.

A highlight of performing in Atlanta was the opportunity to connect with Robert Barnett, Director of Atlanta Ballet, whenever I brought a theater company to the city. Mr. Barnett was a walking ballet encyclopedia, and always ready to share anecdotes and stories.

'Valse Fantasy.' Choreography by Balanchine. Music by Glinka. Set Design by Rick Paul.

I received the above photo, but do not recall who captured the shot. Unfortunately, I didn't take any photos in the last three years of our tours. There was not the luxury of time with the business of traveling to 66 cities a year. We all know how difficult it is to navigate an airport. But imagine 132 flights within six months to complete 66 performances each year.

If anyone has photos of 'Stars' it would be appreciated if you could send. (Some photos from this book are available on my Fine Arts America website.)

'Solstice' was a crowd-pleaser and always closed performances with standing ovations.

The ballet reached a climax when Russell Chambers lifted Phyllis Papa.

Standing on one foot, he lifted Phyllis above his head. Russel held her by one foot as both dancers balanced on one leg while extending the other leg from the hip.

They then both turned multiple times, both in arabesques. The audience was in awe!

(But don't try this at home!)

The set design above is by Rick Paul. Choreography by Steven Simmons. Music: 'Tubular Bells' by Mike Oldfield,

> **THE NEW YORK TIMES, FRIDAY, SEPTEMBER 16, 1977**
>
> **Stars**
>
> The gift of precision movement, the ability to soar, comes not to every dancer. When the dancer of excellence does come along, the dancer with the wondrous ways with leaps and feints and drifts, how lucky for the rest of us. How elegant just to stare and pretend in one's mind one can move that way too.
>
> Not just one but four such stars will be performing their magic movements here Friday and Saturday. On those nights Suzanne Farrell, Patricia McBride, Helgi Tomasson and Peter Martins, the best of the best, will be appearing at the University of Missouri Music Hall. They'll bring such old and new movement celebrations as "Valse-Fantaisie in G Major," "Midsummer Night's Dream Pas de Deux," "Flower Festival at Genzano," "Abyss" and "Fascinatin' Rhythm." A children's matinee on Saturday will feature "Peter and the Wolf."
>
> Tickets for a chance to stare, or simply to enjoy good dancing, are $4-$10. Matinee tickets are half price. Tickets can be bought from the UMKC Box Office, University Center, 5100 Rockhill Road, 276-3705.
>
> Dance magazine calls these evenings "a unique happening...a triumph." Don't miss them.
>
> **Stars of the American Ballet**
> Friday, September 23/8 pm
> Saturday, September 24/2 pm and 8 pm
> Made possible in part by a grant from Mobil Foundation, Inc.
>
> **Mobil**
>
> ©1977 Mobil Corporation

It was special to have a full-page ad in the New York Times. However, corporate ads did not provide financial aid to Stars, but only supported local city arts. Stars was not a resident company of any city; although housed in New York, the country was our home.

The National Endowment grants were allocated directly to theaters for hosting Stars' appearances.

Stars had the longest touring schedule in American dance history, appearing in 66 cities each year.
Every performance sold out with standing ovations and rave reviews.

Children's matinees, Master classes, and Educational lectures were provided for free to American communities. And yet Stars had to close the company.

The reason was American politics:

One artist's work came to the attention of Senator Strom Thurman, who denounced it as anti-religious. The work was in a museum that received grants from the National Endowment for the Arts. Senator Thurman used the photo to justify shutting down the entire Arts program; some programs survived; but the Dance Touring program was cut.

The Dance Program reached the entire the country, especially for regions that had few opportunities to see professional live ballet. 'Stars brought ballet to more cities than any other program in history, but one politician ended the program.

Tying Up

A major problem arose prior to the last tour when Jerome Robbins, choreographer of 'West Side Story' and 'Fiddler on the Roof,' threatened a law suit against Suzanne Farrell and Peter Martins for performing his ballet, 'In G Major,' on Stars tours. (Ironically, Robbins created the ballet for Martins and Farrell.) If memory serves, Martins and Farrell then refused to dance in any of Mr. Robbins' ballets; and Mr. Robbins dropped the lawsuit.

But then came the bombshell! Two weeks before our tour, I received a notification from the law firm of Weiss and Rifkin that Martins and Farrell requested to cancel all their scheduled performances with Stars. Baryshnikov had just joined the New York City Ballet, and Mr. Martins was concerned that he would not be part of the creation of new ballets because of his tours with Stars.

The news was drastic since Martins and Farrell were scheduled for most of our upcoming performances, and other major names were booked many months in advance.

Ironically, the situation was more complicated, as we had just appointed a new Artistic Director, Paul Mejia, who was married to Suzanne Farrell.

It was also a dilemma for the Arts Sponsors because they had to change their souvenir programs, posters, flyers, and ads, as well as disappoint their audiences.

I felt it was not fair to hinder Mr. Martins, and so I engaged Robert Klein of Louis Nizer's law firm to negotiate a quick settlement. Theatre sponsors agreed to accept other stars as replacements, although it harmed their Arts Subscription series. Signing other names on short notice was also a major problem, since marquee names were usually booked a year in advance. To compensate, we added non-American star names, such as Merle Park and Wayne Eagling of the Royal Ballet.

The Third Master Series
of
The University of Nevada, Las Vegas
is proud to present

WAYNE EAGLING
MERLE PARK

Guest Stars,
by arrangement with the General Administrator,
ROYAL OPERA HOUSE,
Covent Garden, London

STARS OF
AMERICAN BALLET

Howard Dando, Founder and Director

With Special Guest Appearance by
Zina Bethune

Karen Hebert • Kimberley Pearce • Carmela Sanders
Cynthia Schowalter • Barbara Weil • Ken Woodson
Manuel Urrego • Roger Rouillier • Lars Rosager
Roland Morrissette

The Third Master Series
of
The University of Nevada, Las Vegas
presents
Wayne Eagling • Merle Park
Stars of American Ballet

'Stars of American Ballet' was a 'loss leader' for Arts Subscription programs. Although that may seem like a negative term, it's not. Customers who wanted to see Martins and Farrell and not have to travel to New York would then purchase the complete Arts Season, that included smaller events like chamber or solo music concerts.

We also signed television star Zina Bethune, best known for the hit series, 'The Nurses,' and TV and Broadway. At 14, she played the role of Clara in the original Balanchine production of 'The Nutcracker.'

Stars' touring schedule was normally a blur of activity, exhaustion, and emotions, but by losing government support, it swept us into a whirlwind. I had to skip our company's Northwestern tour to stay in New York and work on finding financial support and sponsorship to keep the company afloat.

But while I was in New York, two dancers complained they were doing all the work, and they should run the company.

John Starr, our booking agent met with the couple to explain that behind-the-scenes personnel were indispensable, including financial, legal, union contracts, travel logistics, booking agents, publicity agents, accountants, managers, physical properties, royalty rights, and sixty-six theatre contracts each year. When the dancers returned to New York, we met, truths were told, and the dancers were replaced.

But now, without the Dance Touring Program 'Stars' backing us, we could not afford to perform in smaller cities. We needed longer engagements in major cities; and to accomplish this, we needed a 'Superstar.'

To that aim, I met with Margot Fonteyn in her dressing room after a performance. Margo was intrigued by my offer to headline our company, but her schedule was already committed. Charming and modest, Miss Fonteyn even made a comment about her age, "If the audience wanted to see me do thirty-two fouettes, they should have come ten years ago."

I met for business, but her charm was so captivating during our hour-long conversation that everything else faded away, making it a delightful experience.

Stars received other offers, including a month's tour of Asia, and a full week engagement at the Wolf Trap Festival for the Performing Arts. Nonetheless, I rejected the offers because of the formidable challenge of bringing together all the dancers, especially for two non-contiguous engagements.

The curtain closed on Stars, but hopefully this journal will bring back wonderful memories for all those in the company; and the audiences across the country.

WITH GREAT APPRECIATION ... to our Dancers:

Susanne Farrell, Peter Martins, Fernando Bujones, Violette Verdy, Patricia McBride, Jacques D'Amboise, Helgi Tomasson, Cynthia Harvey, Ted Kivett, Karena Brock, Eleanor D'Antuono, Marianna Tcherkassky, Wayne Eagling, Merle Park, Merrill Ashley, Allegra Kent, Kay Mazzo, Keith Martin, Hilda Morales, Lawrence Rhodes, Kirk Peterson, Warren Conover, Veronica Tennant, Zina Bethune, John Prinz, Anne Maria D'Angelo.

Phyllis Papa. Betty Chamberlain, Lynda Kuchera, Charles Maple, George de la Pena, John Sowinski, Lisa Moon, Gigi Nachtsheim, Delilah Shafer, Kimberley Pearce, Mark Mejia, Roberto Medina, Larry Hunt, Meg Gordon, Cathy Contillo, Karen Hebert, Cynthia Showalter, Barbara Weil, Roland Morrisette, Carmela Sanders, Russell Chambers, Thomas Banasiak, Sergio Cal, Manuel Urrego, Roger Rouillier, Ken Woodson, Steve Huber, James Vincent, Lars Rosager, Jerry Turner, Miguel Campaneria.

Thanks to the Stars of American Ballet Staff

Director and Founder...................................... Howard Dando
Artistic Directors... Hilda Morales, Keith Martins, Phyllis Papa, Paul Mejia
Resident Choreographers .... Paul Mejia, Stephen Kirk Simmons
Lighting Designer/Stage Manager.................... Paul Lindsay Butler
Administrative Manager ... Cameron Harper
Company Manager.. Michael Meagher
Legal.. Robert Klein, Gene Klein, Louis Nizer & Co.
Accountant... Bert Schneiderman
Set and Costume Design................................. Rick Paul
Head Shot Photography................................... Kenn Duncan
Printing... Artcraft Lithograph, Inc.
Costumes... Grace Costumes; Orfe Costumes
Headpiece Construction ...   George Potts
Sound... Hagen's Sound, Inc.
Teachers.. William Dollar, Vicky Simon, Sara Leland, Airi Henninger Paul Russel, Patricia Stander
Rehearsal Studios.. The Ballet School & Harkness Studios
Rehearsal Pianist... Linda Pelrine
Transportation.. Travel Time, Inc., & Troubadour Travel
Tour Direction... Barry Weissler, John Starr, National Artists Management

Special Thanks

My father was not a dance fan, but he partially financed the first tour. Fortunately, revenues repaid the loan in a few months.

Robert Klein: 'Stars' was originally represented by Gene Klein, Senior Partner of the prestigious Louis Nizer firm, but Gene's son Robert was an avid ballet fan who volunteered to represent Stars on a Pro Bono basis. We became close friends and spoke almost every night; while Bob's wife, Georgeann, graciously supported time with Bob on behalf of the dance company.

Cameron Harper: The Company Administrative Director held the fort in our New York office while the company toured. Cameron's responsibilities in the office did not provide time for her to see the company on tour, but she loved the dancers and was always available to aid a dancer with any problem, and there was no problem beyond her capacity to solve in a most graceful and caring manner.

Everyone loved her. It was a sad day when I told 'Cami' that Stars was closing. We hugged and tried not to cry. Cami was the best of the best.

Paul Lindsay Butler: Our Production Manager kept it all together for every performance and maintained a standard of technical production at the same level for every year at 66 different theatres with different Stage Managers and Crews across the country. It astounded that in hundreds of theatres with only hours to set the stage; he was never late for a curtain call or missed a cue.

John Starr, our Booking Agent, had Stars traipsing back and forth across the country, but his heart was with Stars of American Ballet. He could not publicly admit it since he represented other theatres and arts companies, but he was most proud to represent Stars.

We stand on the shoulders of those who have gone before us, but we are also influenced by the people who we rubbed shoulders. I had the good fortune of associations with Pennsylvania Ballet, Fusion Dance, Les Grands Ballets Canadiens, American Dance Festival, Playhouse in the Park, the New World Ballet, and several Broadway productions, and associations with: Martha Graham, Agnes de Mille, Rebecca Harkness, Paul Taylor, Merce Cunningham, Vincente Nebrada, Murray Louis, Erick Hawkins, John Butler, Lynn Seymour, Oscar Araiz, Peter Gennaro, Fernand Nault, Edward Villella, Jose Greco, Kathy Posin, Dan Mejica, Paul Mejia, Geoffrey Holder, Arthur Mitchell, Robert Rodham, Robert Barnett, and Norbert Vesak

.

George Balanchine: No one was more influential in the world of dance.

I was always hesitant to ask Mr. Balanchine if 'Stars of American Ballet' could perform his ballets, but every time I asked, he would wave his hand and say, " You have wonderful dancers! Please, you take, you take!"

Once I watched a rehearsal as he gave a correction to simply a step. After, he mentioned to me, "You see how less is more?" When a genius speaks, one listens. It influenced my direction in the arts.

Arthur Mitchell. Mr. Balanchine's kindness also influenced his other dancers.

Stars was rehearsing Balanchine's 'Agon' with tape, but we needed the score to perform with a symphony. But the score was difficult to acquire.

I recalled that Dance Theatre of Harlem performed the work and would likely have the score.

I called Arthur and asked if I could go up to Harlem and pick up the score.

But Arthur rushed from his Harlem studio to deliver the 'Agon' score to us at Lincoln Center, an example of dancers supporting dancers.

Balanchine created 'Agon' in 1957 for Arthur Mitchell and Diana Adams. Regrettably, there were complaints about a black dancer partnering with a white woman, but Balanchine refused to change the pairing.

The couple was denied performing on commercial television in the United States until many years later, in 1968, when their performance aired on Johnny Carson's 'Tonight Show.'

Balanchine famously quoted that "Ballet is woman!" Women not only danced, but many of the following women choreographed and even created their own ballet companies.

Martha Graham: Miss Graham is recognized as the most important creator of American Modern Dance. I was producing the American Dance Festival at the Walnut Street Theatre in Philadelphia, a weekly series with six major modern choreographers, including the Graham Company. Miss Graham was well aware of her stature and carried herself as a Greek goddess, a Medusa; and even quoted that "Dancers were the Messengers of the gods." We were in the lighting booth at a rehearsal; and she was displeased with the Lighting Designer and turned to me, "Howard, is it the concept to have the dancers in the dark?" The lighting designer snapped to make quick changes, but her words would be remembered.

Agnes De Mille: In my last semester in grad school, I was also managing the Pennsylvania Ballet when Miss De Mille arrived to choreograph one of her ballets. In college, I danced in 'Oklahoma' and could never have imagined meeting the legend who created the ballets in 'Oklahoma' that opened the doors to more ballet in musical theatre.

I went to a rehearsal to take a photo of Miss De Mille; however, I was hesitant to take the shot because I was first surprised to see her in a wheelchair, but then she was also angry about the lack of emotions from four 18-year-old corps dancers. Ms. De Mille called them to come to her and gave them the following notes: "You girls are just doing the steps! You have no passion, no emotion, and no sensuality! I suggest you all go out tonight, find some boys, and ..."

Rebekah Harkness: Miss Harkness was a composer, socialite, sculptor, and philanthropist but most known as a dance patron, and for creating the Harkness Ballet. She was the heiress to Standard Oil, and quite generous in that both Stars of American Ballet and later the New World Ballet rehearsed for many years in the beautiful studios she created from a mansion on the Upper East Side of New York. I met her occasionally at the studio but always feeling sympathy that, despite being one of the richest women in the world, suffered from a fatal disease.

The Harkness Ballet was an exciting company, but shut its doors after only a few years of existence. Ironically, many of her dancers later joined the Stars of American Ballet.

Miss Harkness also built a theatre on the Upper West Side as a temple for dance, but the theatre closed after a few years with some criticism over the theatre's overly Baroque interior décor.

Lucia Chase: Miss Chase was also an heiress, with the ambition from childhood to be an actress, but took some dance lessons and became a professional dancer and even a dancer with the company she created, American Ballet Theatre.

As the Director of American Ballet Theatre, she did everything right. She collected the best dancers, whether Russian, French, British or American, and with designer Oliver Smith, selected imaginative choreographers to create one of the most acclaimed dance companies. Bravo!

Miss Chase was quite regal, and I noted that many times when we passed each other, and I was wearing a suit and tie, she would smile and say "Hello." But when I wore a sport coat and no tie, she would only nod.

It was also related that Miss Chase was not pleased that I named my dance company 'Stars of American Ballet,' She thought it was too close to 'American Ballet Theatre,' but the name was an accurate representation of the American stars that were from both American Ballet Theatre and New York City Ballet.

Years later, other companies have used the name 'Stars of American Ballet', including a company that reported that they were the first American company to appear in South Africa. Nonetheless, one South African critic made a point of remembering and documenting that the original 'Stars' company had actually debuted many years prior, that played a pivotal role in shattering the apartheid barriers.

Ludmilla Chiriaeff:

I had the pleasure of working with Ludmilla for the two years we toured 'Tommy.'

As a child, she was confined to a Nazi labor camp because of her Russian-Jewish ancestry; but she became a dancer and then Artistic Director of Les Grands Ballets Canadiens and created an astonishing 300 ballets. Fernando Nault was the choreographer of 'Tommy.'

Our tours were during the hippy period and at curtain calls, the audience members often threw joints for curtain calls instead of flowers. The controversial poster was also a departure from the normal Broadway poster or Playbill designs of the time.

Barbara Weisberger:

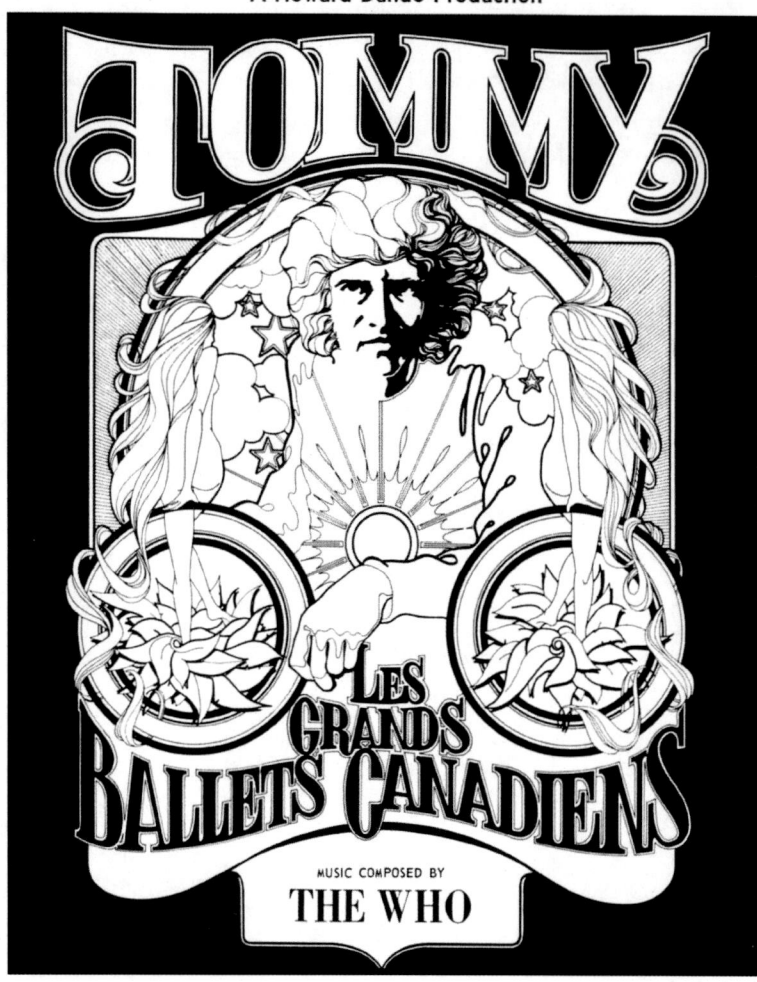

Barbara Weisberger was awarded a Rockefeller grant to create the Pennsylvania Ballet (the name recently changed to Philadelphia Ballet) and from out of nowhere built a company that now ranks in the top of American ballet companies.

My association with Barbara began when I was a stagehand for their 'Nutcracker.' A year later, I was hired as the company Managing Director during my last year of theatre grad school. Somehow, I did both and learned about the logistics of touring. During my time with the Pennsylvania Ballet, were 'bus and truck.' In contrast, 'Tommy' traveled in a 'private' commercial airliner for every city on tour. Both experiences in the logistics of touring helped establish contacts with theatre managers and art sponsors across the country that later provided the foundation to create 'Stars of American Ballet.'

Above and Beyond ...

Eleanor D'Anutono: Eleanor was paired with Fernando Bujones for a performance in Buffalo, but on a day that was hit by one of their worst blizzards. Eleanor was performing with the Royal Ballet in London, but instead of comfortably staying in London, Eleanor caught the last plane that could land in Buffalo A super trouper!

I first met Fernando Bujones on what was his first professional performance at the small barn in Jacob's Pillow. Hilda Morales gave me a heads-up that there was something remarkable I was about to witness. And it was!

After the performance I asked Hilda," "Did I just witness the greatest male dancer in the world?"

Years later, as Director of Miami's 'New World Ballet,' I wanted to pair Fernando Bujones with Cynthia Gregory. Their technique was unparalleled, making them both stand out in dance history.

However, American Ballet Theatre would not release Cynthia from her exclusive contract; a legal battle ensued that was covered by the New York Times.

Cynthia won the case and was freed to be paired with Fernando for their debut with the New World Ballet.

The ABC production of Stars of American Ballet was shot early in the morning because ABC had a dispute with the musicians' union.

For history's sake, I posted a brief clip on YouTube; but not in the original one inch tape but recorded from television in VHS.

(DVD cover)

Paul Mejia became our new Artistic Director during a tough year for 'Stars,' but his calm and professionalism were a major factor in the success of the last tour.

Paul and Suzanne were perceived as being very serious. But prior to our last tour, that myth was dispelled when I was at their apartment and we played a game of Foosball. We competed like madcap maniacs and never stopped laughing for hours.

Suzanne Farrell was a rock star at every performance in every city, but one morning before a performance, we learned that Peter Martins was injured and could not perform. Without both marquee names, the audience might request refunds and the theatre might request a lower fee.

However, Suzanne presented the idea of performing 'Bolero' (a work created for her by Maurice Bejart). The work was not in our repertoire, but Suzanne responded that the ballet was essentially a solo and all she needed was a table; and that she could teach the men in the company their choreography in a couple of hours, since it was the repetition of the same few steps.

I watched from the wings as Suzanne danced on a table for twenty minutes. It was a performance that was mesmerizing. It was clear why Suzanne Farrell was Balanchine's muse. The audience exploded with a standing ovation that seemed to last forever. There are moments in my life that are overwhelming, such as first seeing Michelangelo's 'Pieta;' or Balanchine's perfect 'Concerto Barocco;' or seeing Margot Fonteyn in 'Romeo and Juliet' with Nureyev at the Metropolitan Opera House with a standing ovation that lasted a half-hour (reported in NY Times). Suzanne's performance was up there with those memories.

West Coast Premiere of the Spectacular

STARS OF AMERICAN BALLET

Saturday, October 22, 1977, at 8:30 p.m.
Sunday, October 23, 1977, at 2:30 p.m.

Suzanne Farrell and **Peter Martins,** leading dancers of George Balanchine's New York City Ballet, and **Fernando Bujones** and **Marianna Tcherkassky,** principal dancers with American Ballet Theatre, in ballets and pas de deux by Balanchine, Anthony Tudor, William Dollar and Marius Petipa.

AMBASSADOR AUDITORIUM
Pasadena

ADVENTURES

As we were in the progress of forming Stars of American Ballet, we were involved in another political adventure.

Alicia Alonso was to appear for an engagement in North America, but only in Montreal because her company, Ballet Nacional de Cuba, was banned from performing in America by the United States government. The Cuban ballet star was Alicia Alonso, considered as one of the major ballerinas in history. For the Montreal engagement, she would be in her fifties, an age well beyond most ballet dancers; and she was also practically blind. She had a detached retina; and after several surgeries, spent a year in bed with her eyes bandaged , not able to move her head, laugh or cry.

I thought this was worthy of a documentary and received Cuban permission. I related this to Randy Schwartz, Manager of the Walnut Street Theatre. We were presenting a weekly residency program with six major dance companies; Randy was also a pilot and offered to fly three of our dancers, Hilda Morales, Roberto Rivera, and Alba Casarez. The flight to Montreal was delightful, and we made one stop at the Kodak facility in Rochester, NY to pick up 16mm film.

From the wings, I watched Miss Alonso prepare for performance by going on her hands and knees across the stage to feel for any problems with the flooring; she also needed small lights across the stage apron so she could tell where was the front of the stage.

Just as we were about to interview Miss Alonso, the Russian KGB burst in and halted the filming, prohibiting the interview. They claimed our intention was to use the documentary as anti-Russian propaganda.

That was very disappointing and startling, but there was more intrigue.

Dancers from different countries quickly get to know each other and trade gossip. Azari Plisetski (brother of Russian Prima Ballerina, Maya Plisetskaya) approached me, as he heard we had an airplane. He related that photography was his hobby, and asked if he could fly with us to take aerial photos. I agreed.

Azari spoke Spanish, and Roberto, one of our dancers, could interpret. At one point, we flew across the New York State border. Azari mentioned if we landed in America, it would be a major political event. I assured him we had no plans to kidnap him; and our only interest was artistic. Interestingly, when we landed back in Montreal, it appeared Azari understood basic English.

But the situation intensified and became a dramatic political incident.

One of the Cuban dancers related to one of our American dancers that he wanted to defect. I cautioned our dancers not to get involved as this was dangerous, since the KGB was watching every move, and during a time of many Russian defectors.

However, the next day, the Cuban Ballet and our dancers were walking on a sidewalk to enter the backstage when a car pulled up, a back door opened and Miguel Campaneria dived headfirst into the back seat; the car then sped straight for the American Embassy.

Miguel initially joined Pennsylvania Ballet and later also joined Stars of American Ballet.

But our adventures were not over. After the last performance, we went directly to the airport since our dancers had a rehearsal the next day. However, there was a violent storm, and ground control forbid clearance to fly. Nonetheless, we headed for the airport with the hope there would be an opening. We were informed at 1 AM that we had been granted clearance for takeoff. I voted to wait until the storm passed; but the dancers insisted they couldn't miss rehearsal. We took off!

For a while, we went through the opening, but then the storm hit. The plane was thrown around like a toy, and we lost radio and heat in the cabin. We also needed to land at Philadelphia Airport for customs search; but we were without radio contact with ground control. We flew in for our landing with a commercial airline only a hundred yards from our tail. Alba's back became cramped, and we had to carry her off the tarmac. And then had to fly to North Philadelphia to return the rented airplane to end our adventure. It is often said there is more drama behind the scenes than on the stage!

We went to Montreal performance since it might be the last chance to see Alicia Alonso perform, although she continued to dance until she was 75 and passed away at 98. She credited her dance artistry by observing all the arts, "A dancer should learn from all the arts. Go to museums and look at the paintings. Everything you do in the arts enriches you."

I snuck two photos, one in performance and the other of the curtain call. Audience members should not do that; but there was more of a concern that the KGB was watching and might confiscate my camera.

Researching the internet for photos of the Montreal engagement, it is possible the two photos seen here for the first time might be the only photos available.

Interestingly, Miss Alonzo had both performed and choreographed for Les Grand Ballets Canadiens, the company that I spent two years touring. And she was also a member of the American Ballet Theatre.

(Azari Plisetski on left).

At the same time as our adventure to Montreal, Randy Schwartz and I were developing a dance program for the Walnut Street Theatre.

It was time to shine a spotlight on the innovations of modern dance.

But the idea was not just having the major modern companies perform - but to have half-week residency programs to provide opportunities for Master classes and public lectures.

The Festival exceeded our expectations. After the initial six weeks, we added the Martha Graham Dance Company!

Walnut Street Theatre Presents
The American Dance Festival
Howard Dando, Producer

A series of America's great contemporary dance companies in programs that encompass a spectrum of styles and repertoire.

DANCE THEATRE OF HARLEM   NOVEMBER 2-3-4

JOSE LIMON DANCE COMPANY   NOVEMBER 5-6-7

MERCE CUNNINGHAM AND COMPANY   MARCH 14-15-16

ALVIN AILEY AMERICAN DANCE THEATRE   MAY 2-3-4

PAUL TAYLOR DANCE COMPANY   MAY 2-3-4

ERIK HAWKINS DANCERS   MAY-5-6-7

Soon after the Festival, I moved back to New York to produce the Broadway production of the Who's rock opera ballet, 'Tommy' with Les Grands Ballets Canadiens.

FUSION

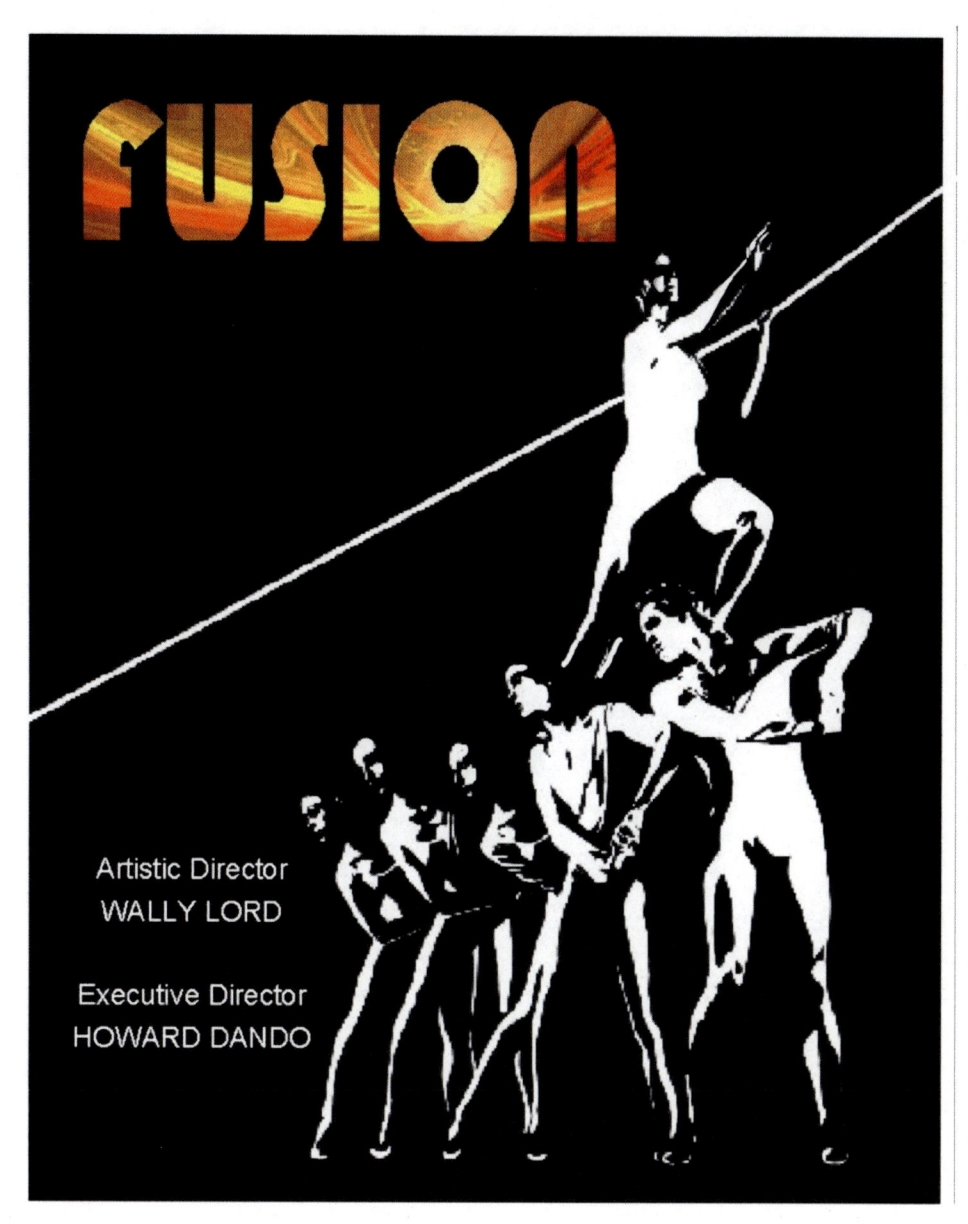

Artistic Director
WALLY LORD

Executive Director
HOWARD DANDO

'Tommy' toured across the country for the next two years

But soon after, I was enticed to go to Miami and guide Fusion, a contemporary dance company, with the anticipation of performing in New York.

The company was struggling with the cost of both rehearsal and theatre space, but I was fortunate to secure a movie sound stage for free by the generosity of Martin Margulies, a Miami real estate magnate and a major art collector.

However, Fusion suffered a major setback when they lost their government funding.

The financial struggles faced by many dance companies led to my interview with Ike Semmens (far right), and John Chancelor on NBC Nightly News.

At this time, there were only three national news stations, so this was significant publicity to advocate other means of support for the arts; including corporate sponsorship.

Fusion escalated publicity with a six-monthly PBS series, radio promotions, magazine and newspaper articles.

The gift of free rehearsal space and a theatre seemed a blessing, but it did not help ticket sales since the company lost its faithful following by moving many miles up north away from its resident home in Coconut Grove.

Fortunately, Fusion would continue as a participant in The New World Festival of the Arts. Unfortunately, the modern dance company would have to compete for an audience against some of the most prominent names and companies in the arts.

Unfortunately, Fusion ceased operations soon after the Festival.

THE NEW WORLD FESTIVAL OF THE ARTS
MUSICAL THEATRE • FILM • BALLET • DANCE • MUSIC
DRAMA • OPERA • PAINTING • DESIGN • SCULPTURE
GREATER MIAMI AND THE BEACHES JUNE 1982

Robert Herman, Director of the Miami Opera, was Managing Director of the Festival; and I was the Artistic Director.

The Festival was sponsored by Miami travel, with the goal of being the largest Arts Festival in the world that hoped to attract visitors to hotels during the summer months.

(New World Festival of the Arts poster by David Hockney.)

Howard Dando
New World Festival Artistic Coordinator

Howard Dando, nationally recognized Broadway producer and former executive director of Miami's Fusion Dance Company, has been named artistic coordinator of the New World Festival of the Arts, scheduled June 4-26, 1982 in Greater Miami.

Conceived as the largest arts extravaganza ever produced in the United States, the Festival will feature world and U.S. premieres of opera, symphonic compositions, plays, a musical, chamber music and dance, offered by outstanding American and international composers, playwrights, lyricists and choreographers. Related events will also include contemporary visual and cinematic arts presentations.

Dando, executive director of the New World Ballet, scheduled to premiere at the Festival, will coordinate the contract negotiations and commissionings for all Festival performances and events. Dando will also act as artistic consultant to New World Festival executive director Robert Herman.

"Dando is well-versed in each of the artistic disciplines," said Herman. "I am particularly pleased to have him working with us. His background and expertise will be an asset to our Festival planning."

Widely recognized for his house record-setting Broadway productions of the Beatles' *Sergeant Pepper's Lonely Hearts Club Band*, and the Who's rock-opera *Tommy*, Dando founded and co-produced the American Dance Festival in Philadelphia and produced the Philadelphia Playhouse-in-the-Park Summer Festival of Music, Dance and Drama in 1970.

In 1970, Dando founded the international touring unit *Stars of American Ballet* which featured such luminaries as Fernando Bujones, Peter Martins and Suzanne Farrell, Violette Verdy, Merle Park and Ivan Nagy.

Howard Dando

In its third year, *Stars* became the fourth most-booked company in America after the American Ballet Theater, New York City Ballet and the Robert Joffrey Company. *Stars* was the first American company to tour South Africa and the first company to perform before a multiracial audience in that country.

Dando's ballet background also includes his managing of the Pennsylvania Ballet Company of Philadelphia.

"I wish to express the gratitude of the Board of Directors of Fusion Dance Company to Howard Dando," said Ronald Platt, chairman of the board for Fusion and senior vice-president of Burger King Corporation.

"His successes this season were not only startling, but his leadership elevated Fusion to its highest level of professionalism. I am delighted we will bring his expertise and substantial experience to the development of the New World Ballet, the New World Festival and the cultural community of South Florida," Platt added.

The New World Festival is estimated to attract attendance of 144,000 and have a $22.5 million impact on the local economy.

AUGUST 1981/SHOWCASE 37

As Artistic Director, I had the dual role as creator of a new ballet company; also to negotiate over 100 new works.

The many original art works included a massive art project by Christo named 'Surrounded Islands'

A new musical by Geoffrey Holder; a new musical by Robert Wright and George Forest ('Kismet,' and 'Grand Hotel'). A Chick Corea jazz chamber music.

Additional works by the Paul Taylor Dance Company, Zubin Mehta and the Israel Philharmonic; and the opening night performance by Lena Horne.

And new plays by Edward Albee, Lanford Wilson and Tennessee Williams.

The plays became very complicated negotiations that were completed only weeks before the Festival.

To negotiate a contract with Tennessee Williams, I drove to his home in Key West; and waited in the garden until Mr. Williams finished his lunch. It seemed a more liquid lunch; as he was in an irritable mood. It was disappointing, since Mr. Williams was one of America's greatest playwrights with Eugene O'Neil, Arthur Miller, and August Wilson. I witnessed a production of the 'Glass Menagerie' when the entire audience leaned forward and were moved to tears as Laura received her heartbreaking news. It was powerful and unforgettable. Unfortunately, Mr. William's play for the Festival was forgettable.

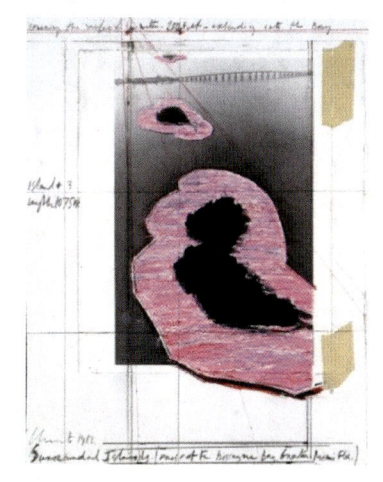

In contrast, the meetings with Christo and his wife, Jeanne-Claude were exhilarating as they sketched designs for their mammoth conceptual project, 'Surrounded Islands.' It was being 'in the room' to witness the creation of art history.

The project was delayed with many approvals from the city with the environmental concerns of sea life.

The final project encircled 11 islands in the bay with 6.5 million square feet of pink fabric.

Despite having talented performers and innovative original works and exhibits, and support from sponsors such as American Airlines, American Express and many cruise ship packages, the New World Festival did not attract a significant audience.

A majority of the arts audience in Miami composed of "snow birds" (commonly referred to residents who sought refuge from the tropical summer heat by traveling to the Hamptons, Berkshires, Fire Island, or Martha's Vineyard, etc.)

Months before the Festival, Ted Griffin, the Festival Manager, proposed to the Board of Directors to postpone the Festival until October. But the goal of the Festival was to fill hotel rooms during the summer.

The only program that sold out was the weeks of performances with the New World Ballet. Newspaper reviews were ecstatic. One reviewer cited if the 'New World Ballet' was on par with, or better than, American Ballet Theatre. Of course not, but we were instantly with the top dance companies of the world - because we had the stars of American Ballet with Cynthia Gregory and Fernando Bujones, and Canadien star, Evelyn Hart and superstar of London's Royal Ballet, Antony Dowell (later director of the Royal Ballet.)

The New York Times reported that Cynthia Gregory sued and won to break her exclusive contract with American Ballet Theatre - just so she could be part of New World Ballet. Brava Cynthia!

A one-hour telecast on ABC TV featured Fernando Bujones, Cynthia Gregory, and members of the New World Ballet.

The New World Ballet enlisted renowned choreographers to produce new original works; however, one work was created by a famous dancer - Lynn Seymour.

Miss Seymour's choreography for 'Rashomon' was based on the Academy Award film by Akira Kurosaw. The story is the rape of a bride and the murder of her samurai husband is recalled from three perspectives: the bandit, the bride, the woodcutter.

It was an impressive work, and notable for the innovative set, (designed by Pamela Marre) that moved with the choreography and the music.

(The ballet included soloist of the New World Ballet: Lori MacPherson, Zane Wilson, Alejandro Menéndez, Naomi Serkin, Svea Eklov, Jocelyne Mocogni, Jim Sutton, Helen Roux, Michel Rahn and Michal Margulies

Apart from a few orchestra rehearsals in Miami, the company rehearsed in New York at Harkness Studios. Ironically, it was a homecoming as 'the 'Stars of American Ballet' came full circle back to Harkness Studios, where 'Stars' rehearsed for many years. A circle within a circle as former members of 'Stars' were now dancing with the 'New World Ballet.'

It took several years after the New World Festival before Miami would have its own ballet company with Director Edward Villella. Ironically, my start in dance was with Edward (and Hilda Morales) for a few engagements. Later, I brought Edward and New York City Ballet dancers to Playhouse in the Park (Philadelphia) that commingled dancers with the Pennsylvania Ballet. Again, what goes around seems to go around.

The purpose of a journal is to relate personal experiences with individuals who have made a difference in one's life. This journal also may serve as a record of important historical events in dance history. (As example, the error mentioned in this journal of another company that claimed they were the first American company to perform in South Africa, but was correctly corrected by one newspaper critic.)

Lori McPherson and Michal Margulies during a rehearsal break.

Fortunately, Harkness Studios has not been converted into prime East Side New York condos; and the beautiful light streaming into the studios will shine for generations of aspiring young dancers.

Moments before the New World Ballet's first performance, I snapped Naomi Sorkin (foreground) and Jocelyne Mocogni, amidst the chaos of their makeup table.

A few minutes later, they were transformed into magical, ethereal creatures on stage.

Yes, 'magical.' The Arts have the power to lift the soul. And make the world a better place.

This photo journal is a personal memory of my association with artists in the dance world. I had many detours with Broadway, Off-Broadway dramatic works, corporate videos, academic and television. But nothing was more inspiring or rewarding than involvement with the arts!

Although there are many distractions, hopefully this journal will serve as a source of encouragement to be engaged in the Arts.

If not a participant, then an audience member, or a donor.

The Pennsylvania ballet (now called 'Philadelphia Ballet') was created by an *'initial'* grant from the Ford Foundation in 1963. The company still exists over 40 years later.

Arts sponsors make a major difference. *Thank you!*

As years pass and memories blur and fade, hopefully this journal may preserve wonderful memories.

Applause to the sponsors across America that sold out every performance and provided their cities with the opportunities to see the best dancers in the world.

Thanks to the critics who applauded in print with hundreds of reviews.

A standing ovation for every dancer who brings to our world their elegance and grace with the beauty and art of dance.

And many curtain calls to all the 'Stars' dancers, and especially the Stars corps de ballet who endured the extensive tours without fame or fortune, but poured their hearts and love to support Stars of American Ballet and the art of ballet.

I am truly grateful.

SAMPLE REVIEWS

"A unique happening, an example of contemporary dance of a standard never seen here. It was a triumph! Powerful interpretation and technical brilliance."   Alan Paterson, Dance Magazine

"The group showed an excellent performance ...it was marvelous!" Anna Kisselgoff, New York Times

"There are some moments that are so exquisite that you wish you could hang onto them forever ... such was the second concert at the Fox Theater."   Atlanta Constitution

"The Crème de la Crème of Dance."   Houston Chronicle

"A superstar company showed what dance is all about, a total visual and sensual dance evening." Pasadena Star-News

"Not just physical virtuosity but a graphic variety ranging from the great Romantic ballets to gripping portrayals in modern dance... graceful, ingenious, intriguing!"   Portland Oregon Journal

"Stars of American Ballet lead the Dance Renaissance."   Denver Post

"A superstar company showed what dance is all about! Pasadena Star-News

"Technical skill and personal magnetism, the index to artistry."   Los Angeles Times.

"Stars of American Ballet is an idea whose time has come! Every dancer was a powerhouse of talent. I lost count of the curtain calls."   Burlington Free Press

"Each member dances truly, freely, brilliantly, and with a joy that is projected into the audience evoking screams of 'Bravo' and prolonged applause seldom heard before."   The Argus, Johannesburg

"A breathtaking performance that brought the capacity audience to its feet."   Richmond News Leader.

"Stars of American Ballet is a company of the cream of American Ballet Companies." Kansas City Star

"The main floor was packed, the dancers were pure poetry."   Emporia Gazette.

"Real stars performing the most difficult art form in apparently effortless style."   The Rock, Greensboro.

"Beauty, grace, control and energy, a company at its 'zenith"   The Dakota

"An Exercise in Grace...ballet buffs certainly got their money's worth. A sell-out crowd interrupted most numbers with applause and greeted several with cries of Bravo!"   Penn State University Mirror.

"Skill, grace and sheer beauty; collectively commendable, singularly superb, Stars of American Ballet gave a truly spectacular performance."   Kansas State Collegian.

"There's no doubt! Stars of American Ballet's brilliant and virtuoso performances are breathtaking." Johannesburg Beeld

"America is the acknowledged world center of ballet. Stars showed how and why." Star, South Africa

Howard Dando

Producer of the original Broadway production of The Who's rock-opera *Tommy* with Les Grand Ballets Canadiens. Producer of Broadway production of the Beatles, *Sgt. Pepper's Lonely Hearts Club Band*. Director of Broadway production, *Elvis, The Legend Lives* (Palace Theatre).

Artistic Director of the City of Miami's New World Festival of the Arts with performances of all new original works of Opera, Symphony, Chamber, Modern Dance, Ballet, and Theatre. Managing Director of Miami's New World Ballet with Cynthia Gregory, Evelyn Hart, Fernando Bujones, and Anthony Dowell. Producer of ABC-TV 'New World Ballet.'

Producer of the American Dance Festival at the Walnut Street Theatre, weekly residencies with the Paul Taylor Company, Alvin Ailey Company, Eric Hawkins Dancers, Jose Limon Company, Dance Theatre of Harlem, Merce Cunningham Company, and Martha Graham Company. Producer. Beacon Theatre NYC.

Director of the City of Philadelphia's Playhouse-in-the-Park Summer Festival of Theatre. Music and Dance. Managing Director of the Pennsylvania Ballet Company, Fusion Dance Company. Producer, Contemporary Music Series at Philadelphia's Academy of Music, Producer: ABC A&E, PBS Miami, and New York. Theatre Professor at four colleges and universities. Author of the novel, 'Dancing with the Devil.'

If you found this book enjoyable
it would be most appreciated
if you could write a review and
share with friends and family.

Made in the USA
Columbia, SC
28 September 2024

a9dd1816-898f-4ec7-a51d-c3c055bf8c66R01